B LAFAYE, ZADRA
Zadra, Dan.
Lafayette : freedom's general (1757-1834   JNB

S0-AAC-988

953538

j B LAFAYE ZADRA
Zadra, Dan.
Lafayette

WITHDRAWN

Property of:

**HUSSEY-MAYFIELD MEMORIAL
PUBLIC LIBRARY**

ZIONSVILLE, INDIANA   46077
(317) 873-3149

GAYLORD

WE
THE PEOPLE
LAFAYETTE

Published by Creative Education, Inc. 123 South
Broad Street, Mankato, Minnesota 56001

Copyright © 1988 by Creative Education, Inc.
International copyrights reserved in all countries.
No part of this book may be reproduced in any form
without written permission from the publisher.
Printed in the United States.

Library of Congress Cataloging-in-Publication Data

Zadra, Dan.
  Lafayette : freedom's general (1757-1834)

  (We the people)
  Summary: An easy-to-read biography of the
French nobleman who was a leader in both the
American and French revolutions.
  1. Lafayette, Marie Joseph Paul Yves Roch
Gilbert Du Motier, marquis de, 1757-1834—
Juvenile literature.   2. Generals—United States—
Biography—Juvenile literature.   3. Generals—
France—Biography—Juvenile literature.
4. United States.   Army—Biography—Juvenile
literature.   [1. Lafayette, Marie Joseph Paul
Yves Roch Gilbert Du Motier, marquis de, 1757-1834.
2. Generals.   3. Statesmen]   I. Keely, John, ill.
II. Brude, Dick, ill.   III. Title.   IV. Series.
E207.L2Z33   1988   944.04′092′4 [B] [92]   87-33259
ISBN 0-88682-190-8

WE
THE PEOPLE
LAFAYETTE

FREEDOM'S GENERAL
(1757-1834)

DAN ZADRA

Illustrated By Jon Keely And Dick Brude

Hussey-Mayfield Memorial
Public Library
Zionsville, IN 46077
953538

CREATIVE EDUCATION

WE
THE PEOPLE
LAFAYETTE

This is not a fairy tale, but it may sound like one. You see, the hero of this story grew up in a castle. He left home at an early age. He fought bravely in several wars and grew to be very rich and famous. Though born in France, he became one of America's greatest patriots—a defender of freedom, and a champion of the poor.

Born in 1757, he was given a long and noble name: Marie Joseph Paul Yves Roch Gilbert du Motier, Mar-

quis de Lafayette. But his friends and family simply called him Gilbert.

When Gilbert was ten years old, he hunted a monstrous wolf that had been terrorizing the countryside. Gilbert felt it was his duty, as lord of the castle, to defend his people against wild beasts and evil-doers.

Gilbert never did catch the wolf. But he grew up feeling that a French nobleman ought to do noble deeds.

Gilbert's father, a soldier, had been killed by a British cannonball before the boy was born. He left his son a small bank account and a tumble-down castle near beautiful Chauvaniac in the French country region of Auvergne.

When Gilbert was eleven, his mother sent him to school in Paris, capital city of France. The young Marquis de Lafayette was dismayed to see the way other noblemen wasted money.

While the King and his court lived in luxury, the poor people of Paris went ragged and hungry. Gilbert was astonished to see old people sleeping in alleys and doorways. He watched in horror as young mothers searched through garbage in hopes of finding a crust of bread for their children. He saw the fear and hopelessness in the eyes of the poor and his heart went out to them.

In 1771, when he was 14, Gilbert went to military school. He wanted to be a soldier, like his father. Then something quite startling occurred. Gilbert received news that his

grandfather had died and left him a huge fortune. Gilbert remembered the poor people of Paris. He resolved to use his new wealth for a worthy purpose—not waste it on fancy clothes, parties and gambling.

In 1774, when he was just 16, Gilbert married the lovely daughter of the Duke d'Ayen.

The Duke wanted his new son-in-law to become a courtier of the French king, Louis XVI. But Lafayette said that court life was phony and pompous. He was a soldier at heart. He went to join his regiment in Belgium.

The next year, Lafayette learned about the American Revolution. As he read the Declaration of Independence, his spirits soared. "Liberty and

equality for all," he exclaimed. He decided to do all in his power to help the American rebels fight the British. He convinced several of his friends to help, too.

Though he was still a teen-ager, Lafayette went directly to an American agent in Paris and boldly asked to be made an officer in the Continental Army. In return, the young marquis promised to fight without pay, and to transport other French soldiers to America. The bargain was sealed.

By a special act of Congress, Lafayette was made a major general. He bought a ship and said good-bye to his young wife. Then he sailed for America in 1777. With him were a number of other French soldiers.

The French volunteers received a surprise when they got to Philadephia. Leaders of the Continental Army, suspicious of their motives, did not want them!

Patiently, and with great dignity, Lafayette managed to convince the leaders that he and his men were sincere in wanting to fight for American freedom.

At the age of 19, Lafayette was confirmed in the rank of major-general. If George Washington was dismayed at the youth of his new officer, he did not show it. Young Lafayette was humble and eager to learn. He did not sneer at the ragged Continental Army, as other foreign soldiers did.

In September, 1777, British

troops began marching toward Philadelphia. Lafayette prepared for his first battle.

The British, commanded by General William Howe, surprised the Americans on Sept. 11 at Bran-

dywine Creek. With muskets blazing, rank after rank of Howe's well-disciplined redcoats descended on the bewildered Americans. Though some of his troops fled in fear, young Lafayette sat firm in the saddle. The

Americans were defeated that day, and Lafayette was wounded in the leg. But he had demonstrated courage and confidence beyond compare.

George Washington was so impressed by the marquis' bravery that he told his doctor: "Treat this man as though he were my son."

Just ten weeks later, before his wound had healed, Lafayette insisted on going into battle again. This time he led a small force against fierce Hessian troops near Gloucester, New Jersey. Using clever strategy, Lafayette routed and defeated the Hessians. He proved that he was a gifted officer as well as a brave man.

Congress rewarded him by giving him command of a division, some

3,000 men. Lafayette joined his men at Valley Forge, early in the winter of 1777. The men had rags for clothing and very little food. Their only shelter against deep snow and bitter cold was a huddle of crude lean-to huts. Lafayette tried in vain to find clothing and food for the men. When none was to be had, he insisted on sharing their hardships.

The American troops called Lafayette "the soldier's friend." Next year, when supplies became available, the young general bought clothes and equipment for his men.

In 1778, France allied herself with America against Britain. Lafayette was filled with joy. After fighting in two more battles, Lafayette suggested that he might go

to France and secure more help for America.

He received a hero's welcome in his native land.

Lafayette was in France for more than a year. He convinced Louis XVI to send money and French fighting men to America. Then, in 1780, he himself returned to America to take up his duties as a general once more.

In 1781, he led troops in skirmishes with the British in Virginia. Lord Charles Cornwallis, the British general, had more than 7,000 men against Lafayette's 1,000. Fortunately, American reinforcements arrived, and the French fleet cut off the British at sea.

Now the huge British force, under Cornwallis, was trapped at Yorktown. The French and American allies laid siege to the town. Lafayette led one of the forces that crushed British resistance. Cornwallis surrendered on October 19, 1781. The Revolutionary War was all but won by America.

Lafayette returned to France once more, where he was hailed as "the hero of two worlds." He continued to act as America's friend until the peace treaty was signed in 1783.

The American Revolution had hardly ended when the French Revolution began. Like the Americans, the common people of France wanted freedom, justice and basic rights for all. But this could never happen so long as King Louis XVI and a few privileged nobles held power. Lafayette was a noble, but he was firmly on the side of the common people. Even so, when mobs tried to kill the King and Queen, Lafayette pleaded that their lives be spared.

For a time, Lafayette was considered a hero of the French Revolution. He spoke out for democratic principles. In 1789, he urged the

French National Assembly to create a bill of rights based on the American Declaration of Independence. Eventually, however, he was branded a traitor to the revolution when he denounced its riots and cruelties.

Many aristocrats, including the King and Queen, were killed by the mobs. Lafayette himself was cast into prison in Austria, and his wealth was taken away. His wife and children were imprisoned in France until George Washington arranged for their release.

From 1792 until 1797, Lafayette was a prisoner. He nearly died in captivity. Finally, when Napoleon came into power, Lafayette was set free.

No longer rich, Lafayette became a farmer. He regained his health but

did not enter French politics again until the dictator, Napoleon, agreed to give France a new constitution. Then, in 1815, Lafayette was elected to the French Chamber of Deputies.

In 1824, Lafayette visited America once more. He was greeted as an adopted citizen, the last surviving general of the American Revolution, the "godfather" of American independence. He stayed for an entire year, traveling all over the United States. Parades and celebrations greeted the 68-year-old Frenchman wherever he went.

When Lafayette died in France in 1834, his grave was covered with American soil.

WE THE PEOPLE SERIES

WOMEN OF AMERICA

CLARA BARTON
JANE ADDAMS
ELIZABETH BLACKWELL
HARRIET TUBMAN
SUSAN B. ANTHONY
DOLLEY MADISON

INDIANS OF AMERICA

GERONIMO
CRAZY HORSE
CHIEF JOSEPH
PONTIAC
SQUANTO
OSCEOLA

FRONTIERSMEN OF AMERICA

DANIEL BOONE
BUFFALO BILL
JIM BRIDGER
FRANCIS MARION
DAVY CROCKETT
KIT CARSON

WAR HEROES OF AMERICA

JOHN PAUL JONES
PAUL REVERE
ROBERT E. LEE
ULYSSES S. GRANT
SAM HOUSTON
LAFAYETTE

EXPLORERS OF AMERICA

COLUMBUS
LEIF ERICSON
DeSOTO
LEWIS AND CLARK
CHAMPLAIN
CORONADO

Hussey-Mayfield Memorial
Public Library
Zionsville, IN 46077

041795